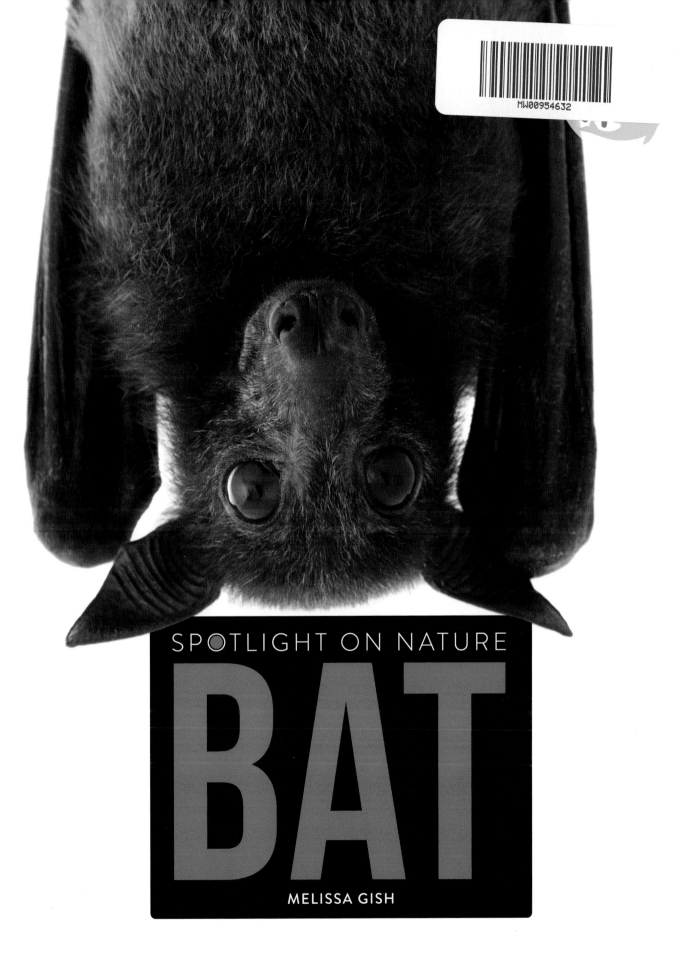

SPOTLIGHT ON NATURE

BAT

MELISSA GISH

CREATIVE EDUCATION · CREATIVE PAPERBACKS

Published by Creative Education and Creative Paperbacks
P.O. Box 227, Mankato, Minnesota 56002
Creative Education and Creative Paperbacks are imprints
of The Creative Company
www.thecreativecompany.us

Design by Chelsey Luther; production by Joe Kahnke
Art direction by Rita Marshall
Printed in the United States of America

Photographs by Alamy (All Canada Photos, Avalon/Photoshot License,
National Geographic Image Collection, Nature Picture Library, Rick & Nora
Bowers, Top-Pics TBK), Dreamstime (Picstudio), iStockphoto (trigga), Joe
Fuhrman Photography, A Matter of Light (Ákos Lumnitzer), Minden Pic-
tures (Ingo Arndt/NPL, Stephen Dalton, Parameswaran Pillai Karunakaran/
FLPA, Chien Lee, Mark MacEwen/NPL, Naskrecki/Guyton/NPL, Konrad
Wothe), National Geographic Creative (JOEL SARTORE - NATIONAL
GEOGRAPHIC PHOTO ARK), Pixabay (paislie), Science Source (Merlin
D. Tuttle), Shutterstock (Rosa Jay, Robyn Mackenzie)

Library of Congress Cataloging-in-Publication Data
Names: Gish, Melissa, author.
Title: Bat / Melissa Gish.
Series: Spotlight on nature.
Includes index.
Summary: A detailed chronology of developmental milestones drives this life
study of bats, including their habitats, physical features, and conservation
measures taken to protect these flying mammals.
Identifiers: LCCN 2019056633 / ISBN 978-1-64026-337-6 (hardcover) /
ISBN 978-1-62832-869-1 (pbk) / 978-1-64000-479-5 (eBook)
Subjects: LCSH: Bats—Juvenile literature.
Classification: LCC QL737.C5 G558 2020 / DDC 599.4—dc23

First Edition HC 9 8 7 6 5 4 3 2 1
First Edition PBK 9 8 7 6 5 4 3 2 1

CONTENTS

SPECTACLED FLYING FOXES
of Halmahera Island

More than 17,000 islands in the Indian and Pacific oceans make up the Republic of Indonesia. The rainforests of one of these islands, Halmahera, are home to the goliath coucal and the **endangered** chattering lory. These birds are found nowhere else on Earth. In the island's swamps, green swallowtails feed on the nectar of guava blossoms, while flightless invisible rails pluck insects from fallen fruit.

It is a late-October evening and a pleasant 78 °F (25.6 °C). The rainy season has come to an end, and cooler air will be moving down from the north. More than 150 feet (45.7 m) above the forest floor, about 20 spectacled flying foxes hang from the branches of a tree known locally as *damar mesegar*. One of the bats begins to stir. The moment she has been anticipating for six months has finally arrived. She is about to give birth to a baby.

CLOSE-UP

Dichromatic vision

Some bats have color-blindness, but
most have dichromatic vision. This means
they can see two of the three primary
colors. However, bats can also see some
ultraviolet colors not visible to humans.

CHAPTER ONE

LIFE BEGINS

Found on every continent except Antarctica, bats are the only mammals capable of flight. More than 1,200 bat species are divided into two main groups: microbats and megabats. Most microbats eat insects, consuming up to 1,000 per hour. Some also eat frogs, birds, fish, and lizards. Microbats have small eyes and large ears because they rely on echolocation to maneuver during flight and capture prey. Megabats have larger eyes and smaller ears. They rely on sight and smell to find food. Megabats eat fruit and flowers, as well as powdery pollen and sugary nectar.

The climate in which bats live often determines their breeding season. Babies, called pups, will be born when food is more abundant.

HALMAHERA ISLAND SPECTACLED FLYING FOX MILESTONES

DAY (1)

- ▸ Born
- ▸ Black fur (dark brown around eyes)
- ▸ Weight: 4.8 ounces (136 g)
- ▸ Length: 2.1 inches (5.3 cm)

Depending on the species, pups can take anywhere from 40 days to 6 months to develop before birth. Microbats are born blind and hairless. Megabats are born furry and with their eyes open. Most female bats have only one pup at a time, though some species can give birth twice per year. A few species have twins. Red bats are able to give birth to three or four pups at a time. Bat pups cling to their mother and drink the milk she produces. Mother bats often carry their offspring when they hunt. Some leave their young clinging to cave walls or trees and in the care of a fellow bat. Mothers are able to identify offspring by their unique vocalizations and scent.

— FEATURED FAMILY —

Welcome to the World

On Halmahera, as the sun dips toward the horizon, the spectacled flying foxes release their grips and flap their wings. They move through the forest in search of ripe fruit. But some of the bats linger in the treetop. They gather around the pregnant female, squeaking excitedly as a tiny pup emerges from her body. She folds her wings around the baby and licks it clean. The male pup is little more than two inches (5.1 cm) long and weighs less than five ounces (142 g).

⑩ DAYS

▸ All milk teeth erupted
▸ Begins flapping wings
▸ Wingspan: 9 inches (22.9 cm)

First Meal

The Halmahera spectacled flying fox pup has found a nipple under his mother's wing. Backward-curving milk teeth help him latch on. He begins to drink his mother's milk. His clawed back feet clutch her fur. Her wings wrap protectively around the pup. She will rest for a few hours. Then she will fly to nearby fig trees and feed on the succulent fruit. Until he is stronger, the pup will cling to his mother as she flies. He will feed on her milk for the first five to six months of his life.

Claws

Bats have four front finger-like bones within each wing. Clawed thumbs are used for climbing and gripping fruit. Five back toes have strong claws that allow bats to securely hang upside down.

Bats have soft fur on their bodies but no fur on their flexible wings. The wings run the length of the body and attach to short hind legs. Some species' wings also attach to a short tail. Bats' hind feet are equipped with sharp claws that help them cling to surfaces. As nocturnal creatures, bats are active at night and rest, or roost, during the day. Microbats typically establish permanent homes in groups called colonies. Most megabat species move between established locations called camps.

 DAYS

    ▸ Can regulate own body temperature
    ▸ Left with babysitter while mother feeds

WEEKS

    ▸ Flies between two close branches
    ▸ Weight: 7 ounces (198 g)
    ▸ Length: 3 inches (7.6 cm)

Echolocation

Microbats use their mouths and noses to make
sounds that vibrate and travel. The sounds bounce
off objects and return to the bats, relaying the size
and distance of objects—even tiny insects. Most
echolocation sounds are too high-pitched for
human hearing to detect.

CHAPTER TWO

EARLY ADVENTURES

For the first 8 to 17 days of a bat pup's life, it cannot regulate its body temperature. Its mother must hold it close to her body to keep it warm. Newborn bat pups can be nearly a quarter of their mother's weight. When a pup becomes too heavy, its mother will leave it behind while she forages. Some species capture insects or bring back nectar or fruit for their young to eat. Pups are born with teeth. Within 10 days, they develop a full set of milk teeth. These teeth fall out and are replaced with up to 38 permanent teeth by the time bats are weaned. Some microbats are weaned within a few weeks, but megabats typically require milk for four to six months. Once they are old enough to hunt, microbats instinctively eat whatever they can catch.

(14) WEEKS

▸ Takes first foraging flight with mother
▸ Licks flower nectar for the first time

Megabats have proven to be as intelligent as dogs. They learn from their mothers where the best fruit and pollen can be found and remember the times of year when certain foods are available.

Most bats cannot take flight from the ground. To take off, they must drop from a height and then flap their wings. Flight style varies by species. Microbats fly slowly but are able to chase and capture darting insects. They can instantly adjust their flight and shift directions while pursuing prey. Some microbats can hover in much the same way as hummingbirds do. Megabats can fly swiftly but are less maneuverable. These bats may journey long distances each night as they forage for fruit, nectar, and other plant matter.

—— FEATURED FAMILY ——

Look Who's Flying

A Halmahera python lounges on a tree branch, watching the spectacled flying foxes that hang from above. The snake's eyes are fixed on the small figure clinging to the mother bat's belly. Now three and a half months old, the pup is ready to leave the safety of his mother's grasp and set out on his first solo flight. If the pup tumbles, the python will lash out and snatch it. The pup's mother stretches her wings. The pup mimics her. Then he uncurls his back toes, releasing his grip on his mother's fur. He falls. The snake braces. But the young flying fox flaps his wings and rises into the air.

⑤ MONTHS

- ▸ First taste of small fruits
- ▸ Weight: 15 ounces (425 g)
- ▸ Length: 4.5 inches (11.4 cm)

Manure packets

Megabats carry seeds in their gut for up to an hour. Then they drop the seeds in their bodily waste. This helps the environment by giving the seeds a chance to grow far from the parent plant.

— FEATURED FAMILY —

Give It a Try

On Halmahera, the juvenile spectacled flying fox has followed his mother more than 10 miles (16.1 km) from the familiar camp trees. His mother leaves him with a dozen other juveniles in a "nursery tree" filled with ripe figs. The youngster plucks a fig with his sharp teeth. He squeezes the fruit between his tongue and the hard roof of his mouth, swallowing the sweet juice. He spits out everything else and reaches for another fig.

MOST **BATS** CANNOT TAKE **FLIGHT** FROM THE GROUND.

(6) **MONTHS**

▸ Fully weaned
▸ Feeds at nursery tree
▸ Wingspan: 2 feet (0.6 m)

CLOSE-UP
Noses

Grooves on a microbat's nose cause sounds to focus in different ways. The more complex a bat's nose, the more detailed the information it receives from echolocation.

CHAPTER THREE

LIFE LESSONS

Bat growth and maturation rates vary greatly by species. Little brown bats become independent at just four weeks, but most flying foxes rely on their mothers for four to six months. Breeding ages also differ. Many female microbats are old enough to breed at nine months, while males may not reach maturity until they are two years old. Female megabats typically mate for the first time when they are two years old. Males breed when they are three or four years old.

Bats are adapted to living in a variety of habitats and eating different foods. The greater bulldog bat has long legs, large feet, and strong, hooked claws suited to grabbing fish. Lesser long-nosed bats feed on nectar deep inside night-blooming saguaro and organ pipe cactus flowers. If bats find themselves on the ground, they are usually

(7) MONTHS	(9) MONTHS
▸ All permanent teeth grown in ▸ Fur around eyes is a pale yellow	▸ Explores neighboring campsites ▸ First roost away from mother

FEATURED FAMILY

This Is How It's Done

Halmahera is experiencing a heat wave. Daytime temperatures continue to climb above 90 °F (32.2 °C). The nearly one-year-old spectacled flying fox has reached his full size. He has remained with his mother's colony. Hanging from a eucalyptus tree branch, he and his family members flap their wings, fanning the air. If the bats can keep from overheating for a few more hours, the setting of the sun will bring lower temperatures, and a cool breeze will drift in from the Halmahera Sea.

in trouble. But vampire bats will actually land on the ground and walk toward their victims. They feed on the blood of animals—mostly cattle—so they typically climb up the foot and bite the ankle. Many bat species need to drink water. They skim the water's surface for a quick sip. For the most part, however, bats stay out of the water. Although they can use their wings and feet to paddle through water, such activity leaves them vulnerable to predators such as crocodiles, fish, and wading birds.

Bats can live from about 14 to more than 30 years. Many bats perish as pups or juveniles. Common predators of young bats include weasels, raccoons, snakes, and even larger bats. Megabats may also be

2 YEARS

▸ Full-grown
▸ Weight: 2.2 pounds (1 kg)
▸ Length: 9 inches (22.9 cm)
▸ Wingspan: 4 feet (1.2 m)

3 YEARS

▸ Joins camp far from birthplace
▸ Mates for the first time

attacked by goannas, which are big, tree-climbing lizards, as well as jungle cats and birds of prey. Small bats may become trapped in spiderwebs. Young bats that fall to the ground will be devoured by any number of creatures—or fungi. By far, however, humans have long been the greatest threat to bats.

CLOSE-UP
Winter rituals

To deal with cold weather, some bats travel to warmer areas. Some microbats enter a form of hibernation called torpor. During torpor, a bat lowers its body temperature and slows its breathing and heart rates.

— FEATURED FAMILY —

Practice Makes Perfect

The rainforests of Halmahera provide an abundance of fruit, which has helped the spectacled flying fox grow healthy and strong. His mother is busy with a new pup and has not been traveling far from the campsite. The three-year-old is eager to explore new corners of the forest. As the sun dips below the treetops, he joins three other young males as they seek new food sources. Soon they will settle in a distant camp and start families of their own.

CHAPTER FOUR

BAT SPOTTING

Bats are easily disturbed, which can spell trouble for them. Cavers or tourists sometimes chase bats from their roosts. Forest-dwelling bats lose their homes when loggers cut down trees. Microbats in cities are often killed or forced from their dwellings. Once bats are uprooted, it can be difficult for them to relocate. Megabats are often considered pests, and people who grow fruit may kill bats that enter their orchards. Pesticides sprayed on crops can kill bats. Others become tangled in nets meant to keep them away from the trees. In some parts of the world, megabats are even hunted for food.

More than 50 different bat species are endangered, and more than 20 others are critically endangered. The Guam flying fox was recently declared extinct. The Livingstone's fruit bat could soon suffer the same fate. It is found only on the two small islands of Anjouan and Mohéli, off the southeastern coast of Africa. Fewer than 1,200 of these bats remain because logging operations are destroying their forest homes. Hibernating bats may fall victim to white-nose syndrome.

Caused by a fungus that grows in cool, moist environments such as caves, this disease can spread from bat to bat. It is believed to have killed millions of bats.

It is possible to save bats, though. In the 1980s, some populations of lesser long-nosed bats declined by as much as 90 percent. Listed as an endangered species, the bat became the focus of conservation efforts by both Mexico and the U.S. By 2018, total population had increased to 200,000. But human efforts may not be enough to help some bat species. As our planet's climate changes, extreme weather events can destroy bat populations. In November 2018, a severe two-day heat wave in northern Australia killed one-third of the nation's spectacled flying foxes—about 23,000—as well as more than 10,000 black flying foxes. Hundreds of pups were orphaned.

Because most bat species are small and remain hidden during the day, they are difficult to study. Scientists use special recording devices to gather information about bats. The North American Society for Bat Research and Bat Conservation International are two major organizations that help universities and conservation programs study bats to learn about their habits and health. Such research can be used to better understand bats and determine ways of preserving bat populations around the world.

SNAPSHOTS

Mouse-tailed bats of the genus *Rinopoma* are the only species with a tail as long as the rest of their body.

Honduran white bats roost on Heliconia plants, chewing the leaves in such a way to create tentlike structures.

The **Bulmer's fruit bat** is the world's most endangered bat. Fewer than 160 adults remain. All roost in one cave in Papua New Guinea.

The oldest bat on record is a **Brandt's bat** that scientists tagged in Siberia and recaptured 41 years later. Such longevity was highly unexpected.

Unlike most bat species, the **Papillose woolly bat** of Southeast Asia lives in family groups, and fathers help care for the young.

The rare **spotted bat** is black with three large white spots. It has the biggest ears of any North American bat.

One of the smallest megabats is the **long-tongued nectar bat**. It has a wingspan of 10 inches (25.4 cm) and weighs about half an ounce (14.2 g).

The **bumblebee bat** is the world's smallest. It is only 1.25 inches (3.2 cm) long and weighs less than a dime.

The three **vampire bat** species of Mexico and Central and South America feed only on blood. Their teeth make a small, V-shaped cut, and they lap up the blood, usually leaving their victims unharmed.

The **Pallas's long-tongued bat**'s tongue is twice the length of its two-inch-long (5.1 cm) body.

The **Mexican free-tailed bat** holds the record for the speediest bat. It can fly as fast as 100 miles (161 km) per hour.

The **lesser short-tailed bat** is found only in New Zealand. Unlike most other bats, it crawls on the ground to find fruit and insects to eat.

The world's largest bat is the **giant golden-crowned flying fox**, which weighs up to 2.6 pounds (1.2 kg) and has a wingspan of more than five feet (1.5 m).

The **northern bat** is the only bat species that can survive north of the Arctic Circle. It hibernates for about nine months of the year in Norwegian caves.

WORDS to Know

adapted   changed to improve the chance of survival in an environment

echolocation   a process to locate and identify objects by emitting high-pitched sounds that reflect off the object and return to the animal's ears or other sensory organs

endangered   at risk of dying out completely

mammals   animals that have a backbone and hair or fur, give birth to live young, and produce milk to feed their young

species   a group of living beings with shared characteristics and the ability to reproduce with one another

ultraviolet   beyond the visible light spectrum at the violet end

weaned   accustomed to food other than milk

LEARN MORE

Books

Niver, Heather Moore. *We Need Bats*. New York: PowerKids Press, 2016.

O'Shaughnessy, Ruth. *Bats After Dark*. New York: Enslow, 2016.

Samuelson, Benjamin O. *Journey of the Bats*. New York: Gareth Stevens, 2018.

Websites

"Bat." San Diego Zoo Animals & Plants. https://animals.sandiegozoo.org/animals/bat.

"Bats." DK Find Out! https://www.dkfindout.com/us/animals-and-nature/bats/.

Harris, Tom. "How Bats Work." How Stuff Works. https://animals.howstuffworks.com/mammals/bats.htm.

Documentaries

Korn-Brzoza, David. *Superbat*. BBC4 and National Geographic, 2008.

Mustill, Tom. "The Bat Man of Mexico." *Natural World*, season 33, episode 6. BBC2, 2014.

Passmore, Greg. *Bats*. Passmore Studios, 2010.

Visit

CARLSBAD CAVERNS NATIONAL PARK

From late May through October, swarms of bats leave the cavern each night.

727 Carlsbad Caverns Highway

Carlsbad, NM 88220

MILLIE MINE BAT CAVE

A self-guided interpretive program and viewing area of about one million bats.

Mine Shaft, Park Ave. off East A St.

Iron Mountain, MI 49801

OLD TUNNEL STATE PARK

Watch more than 3 million bats leave the old railroad tunnel each night (May–October).

10619 Old San Antonio Road

Fredericksburg, TX 78624

YOLO BYPASS WILDLIFE AREA

From June to September, visitors can participate in evening Bat Talks and Walks.

45211 County Road 32B (Chiles Road)

Davis, CA 95618

INDEX